# Puberty: The Game Show

**by Greg Atkins**

**Baker's Plays**
**P.O. Box 699222**
**Quincy, MA 02269-9222**

***Western States Representative***
Samuel French, Inc.
7623 Sunset Blvd.
Hollywood CA 90046

***Canadian Representative***
Samuel French, Ltd.
100 Lombard St., Lower Level
Toronto, M5C 1M3 Canada

# NOTICE



PUBERTY: THE GAME SHOW

*Puberty: The Game Show* was originally performed by students of South Coast Repertory's Young Conservatory Perform Workshop. This workshop production was directed by Greg Atkins.

## CHARACTERS

BABS (BOB) – Extremely efficient stage manager and sound effects expert. Always on top of things and capable of running seven things at once. Can be played by either a male or female.

ALAN – Overly enthusiastic, but not overly genuine, game show host. Looks great ... feels great, but when the cameras are off, looks average ... doesn't feel so hot. When he's on camera, he's the consumate master of ceremonies; making jokes, smiling and keeping the show going.

ELANA – Overly made-up and styled, she is the perfect counterpart to Alan. She is second string to Vanna White with a perkiness that could choke a horse.

KAREN – A pretty twelve year old girl from a divorced family.

TOMMY – Good-looking twelve or thirteen year old boy from New Hampshire. Comes from a close-knit family and is a very "straight arrow" kid.

STUDIO AUDIENCE/ACTORS – This large ensemble of performers must play all of the other characters in the show. When not performing, they sit and react as the studio audience, then, as they are needed, throw on a costume piece and become part of the action. Characters can easily double or triple.

MAKE-UP PERSON
MOTHER – Karen's angry, yet worried, mother.
CHOIR MEMBERS – From Tommy's school.
ROGER– A mean kid.
GIRL 1 and GIRL 2 – Over-the-top commercial actors trying to act like real people.
BEARD HAIRS

NOSE HAIRS
SHAVING KID
MIGUEL – Friend of Tommy.
LARRY – Friend of Tommy.
DWIGHT – Friend of Tommy. Isn't. Thinks he's a big shot. Isn't.
KEVIN – Tommy's nineteen year old brother. Basically a good kid and he actually likes his brother.
MEGAN – Friend of Karen.
AMY
GRETCHEN
KAREN
CAROL
JULIET – The girl who gives Tommy his first kiss.
JULIET'S ARMS – Actor who stands behind Juliet and acts as her arms
TOMMY'S ARMS – Actor who stands behind Tommy and acts as his arms.
BOY
STUDENT 1 – 7
TEACHER
BACTERIA – A group of actors acting like hideous bacteria.
PIMPLE SINGERS – Wearing bathing caps on their heads or white nylons over their faces.
ZIT ZAP PAD SINGERS – Wearing big zit pad costumes.
TOMMY'S INNER VOICE – Stands behind Tommy and speaks what Tommy really feels.
KAREN'S INNER VOICE – Stands behind Karen and speaks what Karen really feels.
KEVIN'S INNER VOICE – Stands behind Kevin and speaks what Kevin really feels.

## PUBERTY: The Game Show

(*Stage right is a double podium where the hosts stand. Hanging up center is a large "Puberty! The Game Show" sign. Stage left are studio audience/actors sitting on risers. The stage is a large colorful gameboard. Perky game show music is heard. Babs is their sound effect expert and stage manager. She wears head phones and carries a clipboard. (If your budget can handle it, put television sets on either side of the stage and have two actors play camera operators with home video cameras. Set up a live feed into the TV's so the audience gets the illusion of a real television show.*)

BABS. Welcome to ... Puberty! (*Applause.*) The show that leads you through the most exciting, frustrating, exhilarating, frightening, and embarrassing time of your life! Puberty! (*More applause.*) Puberty is brought to you by Beard Wacker 2000 Electric Razors. — "Hey, it may look like peach fuzz to everyone else, but it's a beard to Beard Wacker. And Pucker Up ™ — the indelible lipstain that is guaranteed to stay on your lips for an entire month. Pucker Up™ is another youth oriented product from Amway™. And now, the hosts of Puberty! Alan Beckman and Elana King! (*Alan and Elana walk out and take their places behind their podiums. Wild applause.*)

ALAN. Thank you! Thank you everyone!

ELANA. Thanks. (*Applause dies down.*)

ALAN. Well, Elana you look very nice today.

ELANA. So do you, Alan.

ALAN. Oh, this? It's a hand me down from my older brother. (*Laughter.*) I'm used to it. I was thirteen before I got my own toothbrush. (*More laughter.*)

ELANA. (*Laughing.*) Oh, gross.

ALAN. And how about you? I understand you have been very busy.

ELANA. Yes, I've just released my own brand of perfume.

ALAN. You have? Well, congratulations Elana! (*He claps and encourages the studio audience to applaud.*) What is the name of this wonderful fragrance?

ELANA. Elana Wanna. It tells the boys, "Here I am!"

ALAN. (*More applause.*) That sounds great! Are you wearing it now?

ELANA. Yes. (*She pushes her neck out to let him smell her.*)

ALAN. (*Not too pleased with the scent.*) Pungent. Well, I guess we had better get on with it and introduce our first two pre-pubesence contestants.

ELANA. Right you are, Alan. Babs?

BABS. Thank you, Elana. Hailing from Portsmouth, New Hampshire, a state famous for producing Bauxite, please welcome, Tommy Landry. (*Tommy enters to applause.*) And from Oxnard, California, the vacation playground of migrant farm workers, let's put our hands together for Karen Stiver! (*More applause.*)

ALAN. Welcome, welcome. Welcome to Puberty! How are you feeling about embarking on this exciting stage of your life?

KAREN. Fine.

TOMMY. Great!

ALAN. Alright, but before we begin, let's find out a little bit about our contestants. Karen, let's start with you. I understand you are in the seventh grade.

KAREN. Yes I am, Alan. I go to Heinekin Middle School. (*She turns to the studio audience and cheers.*) Go Weevils! (*Her friends do the Weevil cheer.*) My parents are divorced, I live with my mother and see my father on weekends and I have a dog named Bosco and a little brother I hate.

ALAN. Sounds good.

ELANA. And what about you Tommy?

TOMMY. I'm Tommy Landry and I go to Our Lady of Perpetual Motion Catholic School in Portsmouth. I'm in the seventh grade and my school just went co-ed this year, which is okay I guess. My parents have been married for twenty years and I have an older brother, Kevin and a younger sister, Patty. I like computer games and baseball and my best friend is Chuck Heiser. (*He waves.*) Hi, Chuck.

ALAN. Well, it looks like we've got two live ones here, Elana.

ELANA. It sure looks that way, Alan.

ALAN. Are you ready to get on with Puberty!?

KAREN. (*Together with Tommy.*) Yeah!

TOMMY. Let's do it.

ALAN. Alright, let's get you all set up while Elana explains the rules. Elana? (*Alan takes the contestants over to the starting line.*)

ELANA. (*Walking through the game board as she explains the game.*) Thank you, Alan. First stop in our journey is at the starting line and the beginning of the exciting, and, at times, treacherous path of Puberty our contestants must navigate. After picking a card from Alan, our contestants must move the number of spaces designated on the card. Wherever our contestants land on our Puberty Path they must follow the instructions corresponding with the square they land on. Each square holds something new and different for our contestants. Whether it's Most Embarrassing Moments, Hormone Hijinks or My Parents Will Kill Me, every square moves you further along the path of Puberty! And remember, each square give you the opportunity to get Adulthood Points. The more points you get the easier it is to pass through Puberty.

ALAN. Don't forget to mention the Experience Circle.

ELANA. How could I forget that? In order to score extra Adulthood points, the contestants have the option of entering the Experience Circle where they must actually deal with an incident in their growing up process. If they deal with the Experience well, they get those valuable extra points, if they don't they could lose everything. It's a risk, but, hey, what in life isn't a risk?

ALAN. Confusing? Of course it is, it's Puberty!

ELANA. Are we ready, Alan?

ALAN. Are you ever ready for Puberty, Elana? Of course not. But if you're asking if we're ready to play...contestants are you ready to play Puberty!?

KAREN AND TOMMY. Yeah!

ALAN. Then let's get started. (*Game show music from Babs. The contestants go to the starting point, while Alan and Elana go to the podiums.*) And since girls seem to begin Puberty before boys ... who are we to go against nature? Karen you go first. Do you choose the green card or the red card?

KAREN. The red card.

ALAN. Move ahead three squares! (*Applause.*)

ELANA. And you've landed on The Parent Trap. Do you want to go for a three point Question or the six point Experience?

KAREN. I think I'll take the Question to start out with.

ELANA. Alright, here it is. You are asked to the movies by ... Tom Child!

KAREN. I am!?! Oh, my God, oh, my God! (*Shrieks from the Studio Audience.*) He's in ninth grade and on the basketball team!

ELANA. Your Question is: Do your parents let you go?

KAREN. (*A pause.*) Yes, they have to let me go, I'll die if they don't let me go! They have to let me go. Yes, yes!

ALAN. (*Buzzer from Babs.*) So sorry, Karen. They say you're too young to date and anyway the movie was rated NC-17, they'd never have let you in.

KAREN. Oh, my God, I don't believe it.

ELANA. Believe it Karen. No points and move back one square.

KAREN. I hate my parents. I hate them.

ALAN. Of course you do, it's Puberty! Now on to Tommy. Pick a card.

TOMMY. Red, please, Alan.

ALAN. Red it is. And you move one square. (*A smattering of applause.*)

ELANA. You land on Hormone Hijinks. Would you like the three point Question or the six point Experience?

TOMMY. Hormone Hijinks? I better go with the Question.

ELANA. Alright, it's a multiple choice and here it is: Your voice is beginning to change and the first time it happens you are: A – Singing in the shower. B – Talking to the guys after you lost a baseball game. C – Talking to Becky Casey in Math class. Or, D – in front of the entire English class during your oral report?

TOMMY. Ummmm?

ALAN. You only have fifteen seconds, Tommy.

TOMMY. D. During my oral report?

ELANA. (*Bell from Babs.*) That's right! (*Applause.*)

ALAN. Your voice cracks in front of the entire English class during your oral report on Steinbeck's short story, The Hills are like Elephants! Nice job!

ELANA. That's good for three Puberty points.

ALAN. And back to you, Karen. Red or Green?

KAREN. Green.

ALAN. Move ahead one. (*Applause.*)

ELANA. And it's back to The Parent Trap. Experience or Question?

KAREN. I think I'll go for the Experience. (*Applause.*)

ALAN. Then let's go. (*He takes her center stage.*) You know how this works, you get to live the Experience and if the judges feel you have moved ahead in your growing up process, you get the six Puberty points and move into the lead. Got it?

KAREN. Yeah.

ALAN. (*Moving back.*) Take it Elana.

ELANA. Thanks, Alan. Your category is The Parent Trap and your Experience is: Coming Home Late.

KAREN. (*Looking out at the audience.*) Oh, no. (*A Studio audience Member/Mother walks into the Experience Circle. Her hair is in curlers and is wearing a bathrobe and fuzzy slippers.*)

MOTHER. Hello. Or should I say, Good Morning?

KAREN. Mom, I can explain.

MOTHER. 12:16. 12:16 on a school night? When is your curfew?

KAREN. Mom, look I was...

MOTHER. Answer me. When is your curfew?

KAREN. Nine o'clock on week nights, ten o'clock on weekends.

MOTHER. What are you supposed to do if you're going to be late?

KAREN. (*Wearily.*) Call.

MOTHER. It's 12:16, oops, no 12:17. I've checked the phones twice. They work.

KAREN. We didn't leave the library until nine.

MOTHER. So it took you three hours to get home? Were you at the library in Hawaii?

KAREN. Mother!

MOTHER. So where were you?

KAREN. Rachel decided to stop at Jack-in-the-Box for a Coke and when we came out, Doug Willard and some of his friends blocked our car in and wouldn't let us out.

MOTHER. Why didn't you use the drive-thru?

KAREN. Because Rachel was going to drink the Coke then we were going to get a free refill for me.

MOTHER. So why didn't you call?

KAREN. I didn't have any money. That's why we had to get the free refill.

MOTHER. What about the secret ten dollars I gave you to keep in your wallet?

KAREN. (*Looking sheepish.*) I spent it.

MOTHER. On what? I told you to use that money in an emergency.

KAREN. It was an emergency.

MOTHER. What did you spend it on?

KAREN. (*Close to tears.*) Something I needed. You know. (*Not wanting to say it.*) Just something I needed.

MOTHER. Alright, so why didn't you tell me you needed more money?

KAREN. I just forgot.

MOTHER. Karen, look, I want to trust you ...

KAREN. You can.

MOTHER. But you make it so hard sometimes. This is why I won't even entertain the thought of you dating. It has to do with trust and responsibility and maturity. They all three go together. (*Pause.*) So what am I supposed to do?

KAREN. Ground me, I guess.

MOTHER. Yep, I guess you're right. Curfew is now eight o'clock ... (*Karen is about to interrupt, Mother holds up her hand.*) ... don't ... and you are grounded for two weekends.

KAREN. But ...

MOTHER. Three weekends.

KAREN. That's not ...

MOTHER. Four weekends. Wanna try for five? (*Karen doesn't say anything.*) Alright, up to bed. (*Bell from Babs and applause.*)

ALAN. And there's the bell! Good for six points! Congratulations! (*Applause.*)

KAREN. I can't believe it! Grounded for four weekends?

ELANA. Nice work Karen! And we're back to you Tommy. Pick a card.

KAREN. My life is over. (*She sits dejectedly on her square.*)

TOMMY. Green.

ALAN. Move ahead four! (*Applause.*)

ELANA. You've landed on, Embarrassing Moments! (*Applause.*) Question or Experience Circle? And remember you are trailing by three points.

TOMMY. Experience Circle for six points. (*Applause.*)

ALAN. Your category is Embarrassing Moments and your Experience is called: Don't Look Now.

TOMMY. (*Studio audience Members/Choir get in the Circle.*) It's called what? (*Tommy is in the choir configuration. They begin to sing "America".*)

ALL CHOIR.

OH, BEAUTIFUL FOR SPACIOUS SKIES,
FOR AMBER WAVES OF GRAIN
FOR PURPLE MOUNTAINS MAJESTIES,

SOLO.

ABOVE THE FRUITED PLAINS,

ALL CHOIR.

AMERICA, AMERICA,
GOD SHED HIS GRACE ON THEE,

TOMMY. (*Moving forward and we see his shirt tail is sticking out of his fly.*)

AND CROWN THY GOOD WITH BROTHERHOOD,

ALL CHOIR.

FROM SEA TO SHINING SEA. (*Applause.*)

ROGER. (*As the Choir is leaving.*) Hey, dorkbrain.

TOMMY. What do you want, Roger?

ROGER. Nice singin'.

TOMMY. (*Somewhat surprised.*) Thanks.

ROGER. To bad your shirt tail was stickin' out of yer fly.

TOMMY. Oh, my God. (*He turns his back on the audience and fixes his shirt and pants. Bell rings.*)

ALAN. And that's good for six points!

TOMMY. I can't believe that happened! Why did it have to happen to me?

ALAN. We don't have time to dwell on that now Tommy. On to you Karen, red or green.

KAREN. Green.

ALAN. And you get to move ahead three. (*Applause.*)

ELANA. And you land on ... oh, oh, "Mother Finds Your Diary"! ... lose a turn. (*Studio audience "awwwws".*)

KAREN. I can't believe it! This sucks.

ELANA. And one extra weekend of restriction for having a potty mouth.

ALAN. You'd think she'd learn wouldn't you Elana?

ELANA. Yes, Alan, you'd think she would. Well Tommy, here's your chance to really rack up some points.

TOMMY. A red card, please.

ALAN. The red card says, Move three spaces! (*Applause.*) And you've landed on My Parents Will Kill Me. Experience Circle or Question?

TOMMY. I'd better go for the points. Experience Circle.

ALAN. Alright. (*Babs plays music. Alan looks up at Babs.*) Oops. But before we see if you get those big six points, we need to pause for a word from our sponsor. (*Applause. Our Hosts and Contestants, with big smiles on their faces, freeze in place.*)

BABS. And out. (*The Host and Contestants run off stage. Studio audience Member/Actors move downstage for commercial spot. Babs cues Music.*)

GIRL 1. (*Standing with her friend putting on make-up.*) I don't know how you do it, Connie Jo!

GIRL 2. Do what?

GIRL 1. Keep your lipstick looking so great! What's your secret?

GIRL 2. Why it's no secret, it's Pucker Up™ Lipstain.

GIRL 1. Lipstain?

GIRL 2. Yes, Lipstain stays on your lips no matter what happens. Made from the same chemicals used in wood stains, Pucker Up™ colors your lips right down to the third epidermal layer with a permanent, virtually non-toxic petroleum based absorbent dye.

GIRL 1. Can it even withstand Bill Robertson's kisses?

GIRL 2. It can withstand temperatures up to two hundred and seventy degrees Celsius, winds over fifty knots and a windchill factor of minus forty seven degrees.

GIRL 1. Yeah, but can it withstand Bill Robertson's kisses? (*The girls laugh and freeze in place.*)

BABS. Pucker Up ™ Lipstain comes in a rainbow of colors such as: Purple Passion, Simply Red and Pink Nightie. Available at Nordstrom and Toys "R" Us.

(*The Girls cross back to the Studio audience as Babs cues the music for the next commercial. The Studio Audience/Beard Hairs are wearing black construction paper stove pipe hairs on their heads. A Kid stand next to them as if in a split screen.*)

HAIR 1. (*Stretches and yawns.*) Good morning, Steve.

HAIR 2. Good morning, Dave. Hi, Earl.

HAIR 3. Steve. Dave. Hey, you guys are really growing.

HAIR 2. Yeah, you too. We're working on becoming a mustache.

HAIR 3. Really?

HAIR 1. That's what we're hoping to do.

HAIR 3. I'm just happy being a thick black nose hair.

HAIR 1. I can see how you'd be proud, but ... Hey, look!

HAIR 2. Oh, no what's the kid doing?

HAIR 1. It looks like ...

HAIR 3. It can't be ...

HAIR 2. He's picking up the ...

ALL HAIRS. Beard Wacker 2000!!! (*The Kid picks up an electric razor.*)

HAIR 1. It has seventy thousand rotating dual-action blades!

HAIR 2. The first set of blades gently lift us up ... !

HAIR 1. As the second set of blades cut us off ... !

HAIR 2. Giving you a clean, effortless shave ...

HAIR 1. The first time ...

HAIR 2. And everytime! (*The Kid puts the razor to his face.*)

HAIR 1. (*As they are being lifted.*) There's the gentle lifting!

HAIR 2. And now ...

HAIRS 1 AND 2. Ahhhhhhhhhhhh! (*They are cut off.*)

HAIR 3. Bye guys! See ya tomorrow morning!

HAIRS 1 AND 2. (*Muffled.*) Okay!

HAIR 3. Whew! That was close. (*Looking up.*) Hey, wait! What's he doing now? Oh, no, he's using the Nose Wacker attachment for those unsightly nose hairs. (*The Kid uses the Nose attachment.*) Ahhhhhhh! (*He is cut off as the Kid puts the razor down feels his face and checks his nose in the "mirror".*)

KID. (*Looking at the audience.*) The Beard Wacker™ 2000. What a great gift for the fourteen year old boy in your life. (*He holds up the shaver and smiles.*) The Beard Wacker™ 2000 the shaver every boy wants.

BABS. The Beard Wacker ™ 2000 is another fine product from TeenClean, makers of Leg Wacker™ and Pit Wacker™. (*Music fades into game show music.*) Eight, seven, cue the applause, five, four, get ready and ... (*Points to Alan and Elana.*)

ALAN. Hello and we're back!

ELANA. We sure have an exciting game here, Alan.

ALAN. That we do, Elana. What's the score so far?

ELANA. Well, the score now stands, Karen has six points and just landed on Miss a Turn, Tommy has nine points and before our break landed on My Parents Will Kill Me and chose the Experience Circle. So Alan, Tommy has two turns to rack up some major points.

ALAN. Right you are, Elana! So Tommy, are you ready for your Experience Circle?

TOMMY. Yeah, let's go.

ELANA. Your category was My Parents Will Kill Me and your Experience is: Home Alone.

ALAN. Good luck. (*Two Studio Audience/Friends enter the Experience Circle.*)

MIGUEL. So when are your parents and little sister coming back?

TOMMY. Tomorrow.

MIGUEL. And they're letting you stay here by yourself?

TOMMY. Kevin's suppose to be here, but I think he's going to spend the night over at his girlfriend's.

LARRY. It must be so cool to be nineteen.

TOMMY. Trust me Larry, my brother Kevin is anything but cool.

MIGUEL. My parents would never leave me and my brother home alone. They'd make us stay with an aunt or something.

TOMMY. Where's Dwight? He's been in the bathroom forever.

LARRY. Nah, he's out of the bathroom. I saw him on the phone in the kitchen.

TOMMY. He better not be making crank calls on my parents phone. (*Dwight enters with a bottle of vodka.*)

DWIGHT. Lookie what I found in the cupboard!

TOMMY. Dwight, don't even think about it.

DWIGHT. What'sa matter? We have a couple little

drinks, fill it up with water and no ones the wiser. And anyway Jessica, Amy and Philip are coming over with some beer.

TOMMY. When did this happen?

DWIGHT. I just called them.

LARRY. Cool!

MIGUEL. I can't stay real late cuz my mom wants me to ...

TOMMY. I don't know, Dwight.

DWIGHT. Your parents are gone, it's like an unwritten law that you've got to have a party.

LARRY. Yeah, come on.

TOMMY. Shut up, Larry. I didn't say we could have a party.

DWIGHT. People are coming over Tommy, you got to be a real butthead not to let them in.

TOMMY. Dwight, I just finished paying my parents for all of the nine-seven-six phone calls you made the last time you were here.

DWIGHT. Look it's just a few friends.

TOMMY. Yeah, but I know what happens: you call two people and they call ten and eventually the entire town shows up. (*Kevin walks up.*)

DWIGHT. Hey, if you don't want me here, I'll just take my vodka and go.

KEVIN. Funny that looks like the vodka my Dad keeps in the cupboard where if someone is smart they would put it back where they found it.

DWIGHT. Oh, hi, Kevin.

KEVIN. (*Making fun of Dwight.*) Oh, hi, Dwight. Make any interesting nine-seven-six calls lately?

MIGUEL. I gotta go you guys.

LARRY. Me too.

DWIGHT. (*Giving the vodka to Kevin.*) Yeah, I'll walk with you guys.

LARRY. I'll call you later Tommy. (*They exit.*)

KEVIN. That Dwight is a piece of work isn't he?

TOMMY. Yeah.

KEVIN. You know Mom and Dad would have found

out, don't you?

TOMMY. Yeah. I thought you were staying over at Denise's.

KEVIN. Nah, I thought it might be fun to rent a couple of scary movies, get some ice cream, Doritos, and Jolt Cola and do a boys' night sort of thing.

TOMMY. Good idea.

KEVIN. Yeah, I thought so.

TOMMY. You know Kevin, you're pretty cool.

KEVIN. Yeah, I know. (*Bell from Babs and applause.*)

ALAN. And another six points for Tommy! That brings your total up to fifteen! (*Applause.*)

ELANA. How are you feeling?

TOMMY. Exhausted.

ALAN. You don't have time to rest now, because it's your turn again! Red or green?

TOMMY. Green.

ALAN. Move ahead two! (*Applause.*)

ELANA. And you've landed on, Those Magic Moments! (*Applause.*)

ALAN. Question or Experience?

TOMMY. I'd better keep going with the Experiences.

ALAN. Then let's go! (*Applause and Alan hands Tommy a baseball mitt. Tommy enters the Experience Circle and looks up.*)

TOMMY. Oh, my God! Here it comes, here it comes. I gotta catch it. If I catch this we win. If I drop it we lose. Keep calm, don't panic. It's just a game. Just a game. Just the difference between being a social outcast and a hero. Ahh, it's in the sun. Where is it? Where is it? Ahhhh! There it is! Come on, baby! (*He follows the ball down and catches it.*) I did it! Alright. (*The bell rings, then Tommy drops the ball.*) Oh, no! (*The Buzzer.*)

ALAN. Oh, too bad Tommy! No points.

TOMMY. I'm gonna be a social defect. No one on the team will ever talk to me again.

ELANA. We all thought you had it.

TOMMY. So did I.

ALAN. Well, we can only imagine the ridicule and

embarrassment you are going to have to endure for the rest of your life because of one simple little mistake like dropping the ball in the final game of the Little League Championships.

ELANA. Luckily we can only imagine it, you have to live with it. Now, on to Karen!

ALAN. Red or Green, Karen?

KAREN. Green.

ALAN. And it's a big move five spaces! (*Applause and the Studio audience counts as she walks.*)

ELANA. You've landed on Girls Together. Question or Experience?

ALAN. And let us remind you that you are nine points behind Tommy. Now is a good time to go for the big points.

KAREN. I guess I'll have to go for the Experience.

ALAN. Alright, this is for six points.

ELANA. Karen, your category is Girls Together and your Experience is: Slumber Party.

KAREN. How fun! (*The Studio Audience/Slumber Partiers wearing robes, carrying pillows, stuffed animals, chips, popcorn, etc. move into the Experience Circle. They sit.*)

MEGAN. Okay, Gretchen it's your turn. Truth or Dare?

GRETCHEN. Truth.

MEGAN. Okay, (*She thinks.*) did you, or did you not French kiss Chris Best on the team bus on the way back from the game against Riverside?

AMY. Yeah! And tell the truth this time.

GRETCHEN. I didn't lie last time.

CAROL. Yeah, sure.

MEGAN. Answer the question.

GRETCHEN. Alright, yes! Yes I did!

KAREN. Oh, gross.

GRETCHEN. It was not!

CAROL. Admit it, Gretchen, I mean ... Chris Best?

GRETCHEN. Who's turn is it now?

MEGAN. Okay, Amy it's your turn.

GRETCHEN. It's Carol's turn.

MEGAN. It's my house and I get to make up the rules and I say it's Amy's turn.

GRETCHEN. Some hostess.

MEGAN. Okay Amy, Truth or Dare?

AMY. Dare.

KAREN. Amy it's no fun if you always take the Dare.

AMY. Who says?

MEGAN. Okay, Amy ... (*She hands Amy a piece of aluminium foil.*), chew on this aluminium foil for thirty seconds.)

ALL. Euwwwwwww!

CAROL. Oh, God you have all of those fillings!

AMY. I don't want to chew it.

MEGAN. It doesn't matter, you chose Dare so start chewing. (*Amy takes the foil and begins chewing. Megan times her.*) Five seconds. Ten seconds. Fifteen seconds.

AMY. (*Grimacing.*) This is awful.

ALL. Ahhhhhh!

MEGAN. Twenty seconds.

AMY. I'm going to spit it out.

MEGAN. If you do, after you fall asleep we're going to put your hand in warm water and you'll pee the bed.

KAREN. Keep chewing, I'm sleeping next to you.

AMY. Ahhhhh!!

MEGAN. Five, four, three, two, one.

ALLY. Yea!! (*Amy spits the foil out.*)

AMY. Oh, my God, that feels so disgusting. It hurts your teeth so bad.

MEGAN. Maybe next time you'll pick Truth. Okay Karen, your turn, Truth or Dare?

KAREN. Megan, it should be Carols turn next. She has to leave soon.

CAROL. Yeah, my brother's picking me up.

MEGAN. You mean the brother that Karen is in "love" with.

KAREN. I am not.

MEGAN. You are too.

AMY. You are too, Karen.

CAROL. (*Sing-song.*) Karen and David sitting in a tree,

K-I-S-S-I-N-G, first comes love, then comes marriage, then comes a baby in a baby carriage!

KAREN. Carol!

MEGAN. It's written all over your face every time you see him at lunch.

KAREN. It is not.

MEGAN. Okay, let's see if it is true. Truth or Dare?

KAREN. Dare.

MEGAN. Chicken.

AMY. You might as well do Truth, Karen.

KAREN. I said Dare.

MEGAN. Okay, (*she pulls out a roll of toilet paper.*) stuff this toilet paper in your bra until you are as big as Dolly Parton.

KAREN. Gross!

ALL. Do it! Go on. Etc. (*Karen begins stuffing her top.*)

MEGAN. They need to be bigger.

KAREN. Then why don't you show me how to do it.

MEGAN. Okay. (*She begins to stuff her top. Soon everyone is getting into the act: stuffing their tops, dancing, bumping into each other, laughing, etc. David walks in. All but Karen see him and stop.*)

KAREN. (*Puffed up twice the size of Dolly Parton, still doesn't see David.*) What's the matter? (*Amy points to David. Karen turns, sees him, then wants to die.*)

DAVID. Are you ready to go, Carol?

CAROL. Yeah, let me get my things. (*She pulls a stuffed bear out from her blouse.*)

AMY. I wish you could stay the night, Carol.

CAROL. We gotta go to see my Dad. It's his weekend. (*Grabbing her stuff.*) I'll call you guys later. Thanks for having me over Megan. (*All ad lib goodbyes. Carol walks off.*)

MEGAN. Bye, David.

DAVID. Bye, Megan. Bye, Amy. Bye, Gretchen. Bye, Karen. (*He starts to go, then stops.*) Say Karen, there's something different about you but I can't figure out what it is. (*He pauses.*) Get a new hairdo? (*He smiles and leaves.*)

KAREN. I want to die.

ALAN. And that is good for six points! (*The Girls exit and the Studio audience applauds.*)

KAREN. My life is over. (*To Alan.*) Does anything good happen on this show?

ALAN. Back to you, Tommy. Let me remind you that you are only three points ahead of Karen so pick a good card.

TOMMY. Red.

ALAN. You move two spaces!

ELANA. And land on First Love! (*Applause.*) Question or Experience?

TOMMY. Well, Elana I guess I've got to go for the six point Experience.

ELANA. Alright, your category is First Love and your Experience is: First Kiss.

TOMMY. First kiss!?! Oh, man this stuff makes me nervous.

ALAN. So head on over to the Experience Circle.

(*Two studio audience Members/Arms move in behind Tommy and Juliet. Tommy and Juliet put their hands behind their backs and the "arm" actors slip their arms through so that they become the arms of the actors in front. Tommy and Juliet act out the scene while the Arm Actors provide all of the arm movements. The Arms hold hands and the actors and Arms stroll into the Experience Circle.*)

TOMMY. So you liked the movie?

JULIET. (*Smiling.*) I've told you four times, I liked the movie. Why are you acting so weird?

TOMMY. I don't know, (*pulling his hand away.*) I feel really uncoordinated tonight.

JULIET. (*Taking his hand back.*) Why?

TOMMY. I guess because it's our first date and I want everything to be perfect. (*He runs his hand through his hair.*)

JULIET. It has been perfect. (*She opens her purse and puts on lipstick. He watches her.*) Well, here we are.

TOMMY. Yes. Yes, here we are. (*There is an uncomfortable pause.*)

JULIET. I had a wonderful time tonight.

TOMMY. So did I.

JULIET. I'd like to do it again.

TOMMY. You would?

JULIET. Yes.

TOMMY. Okay. (*They start to kiss. The arms can't figure out which way to hold each other. Babs flashes a flashlight on and off. Suddenly Tommy jumps back.*)

JULIET. It's okay, it's just my mom flicking the porch light off and on. It means I have to go in.

TOMMY. Oh, well then, goodnight. (*He starts to leave.*)

JULIET. (*Her hand grabs his.*) Hey, didn't you forget something? (*She pulls him to her and they kiss. Babs flashes the flashlight. Tommy pulls back though he is still holding her hands. Juliet sighs.*) I'll be in in a minute, Mother! (*To Tommy.*) I better go.

TOMMY. Me too.

JULIET. Call me tomorrow.

TOMMY. Okay, 'night.

JULIET. 'Night and thanks. (*She exits the circle. Tommy's arms punch the air and clap his hands.*)

TOMMY. Oh, yes!

ALAN. And another six points for Tommy! (*Applause.*)

ELANA. And time for another word from our sponsors. (*Ad lib congratulations into ...*)

BABS. And out. (*Studio Audience Member/Students sit on chairs downstage. Student 2 has her arm raised.*) Has this ever happened to you?

STUDENT 1. Hey, put your arm down.

STUDENT 2. Why? I know the answer.

STUDENT 3. 'Cause you have B.O. that could kill a gym teacher.

STUDENT 2. I do not.

STUDENT 1. Do you ever wonder why no one ever talks to you?

STUDENT 2. Or eats lunch with you?

STUDENT 4. Or runs gagging from the classroom when you enter?

STUDENT 3. I thought it was my personality.

STUDENT 1. Not in this instance.

STUDENT 3. What can I do?

STUDENT 4. Have you tried, Passion Pit, the antiperspirant that makes your armpit smell like a flower shop? It's what all of us active teens wear.

BABS. (*As Announcer.*) Yes, with Passion Pit you can raise your arm with confidence. (*Studio audience Member/Bacteria moves forward.*) Here is an armpit odor bacteria magnified five billion time it's actual size to show you how repulsive they can be. Now imagine millions and millions of these bacteria ... living, breathing, shopping and working in your moist armpit. Disgusting isn't it. So, whether it's roll-on, stick, pads, spray or gel, show everyone at school that you can have brains and be sweet smelling too by using Passion Pit.

STUDENT 2. (*Whispering.*) You know the answer to *that* question!?!

STUDENT 3. No. I just like to raise my arm with confidence.

BABS. (*As Teacher.*) Yes, Miss Gibson what is the atomic weight of hydrogen? (*Student 3 pulls her arm down quickly.*)

STUDENT 3. (*To the audience.*) Sometimes you can be too confident!

BABS. (*As Announcer.*) Passion Pit, the antiperspirant that gives you the confidence to raise your hand ... even if you don't know the answer. (*The Students leave. Music plays as the Pimples come downstage.*)

PIMPLE SINGERS. (*Singing.*)

WE ARE YOUR PIMPLES

WE LIVE UPON YOUR FACE
WE ARE HAPPY PIMPLES
YOU'LL FIND US EVERY PLACE

WE ARE NASTY PIMPLES
YOU'LL NEVER GET RID OF US
WE ARE PUSS FILLED PIMPLES
THAT ERUPT LIKE VESUVIUS

ZIT ZAP PAD. (*Spoken.*) Not so fast! (*The Zit Zap Pads come running down and surround the Pimples.*)

ZIT ZAP PAD SINGERS. (*Singing.*)
WHAT YOU NEED IS A ZIT ZAP PAD
THE BEST FRIEND YOU EVER HAD
JUST WIPE IT ALL ALONG YOUR FACE
AND PIMPLES LEAVE WITHOUT A TRACE

NOW THAT YOUR SKIN IS LOOKING HOT
YOU CAN GO BACK TO EATING CHOC-O-LATE,
FRIES, AND CHIPS AND ALL THINGS BAD
JUST THANK YOUR HANDY ZIT ZAP PAD.

BABS. Zit Zap Pads come in Padettes, Extra Strength Pads, and full body wraps. From Amway. (*Applause.*) And we're back in five, four, get ready, two and ... (*Babs points to Alan.*)

ALAN. Well, Elana we're almost through Puberty. Boy, what an exciting show we're having today.

ELANA. That's right, Alan. As the score now stands: it's Karen with twelve points and Tommy with twenty-one and it's Karen's turn.

ALAN. Right you are. Karen pick a card, if you please.

KAREN. I pick green, Alan.

ALAN. And that's good for two spaces. And you land on ... Move Ahead three! (*Applause.*) What a lucky break for Karen. Moving ahead three puts you on Why Me?

KAREN. Why Me?

ALAN. That's correct.

KAREN. I don't know. Why Me? I think I'll go with the Question.

ALAN. The Experience is worth six points, but you're

the boss. If you get it right this three point Question will bring your score up to fifteen.

ELANA. And your Question is: Does your mom get remarried again?

KAREN. Oh, no! I bet she does. I bet she's going to marry that Richard guy. Oh, no!

ALAN. Right you are! Three points!

ELANA. You're mother does marry Richard and after a year of writing really bad teenage girl poetry about it and making everyone's lives miserable, you realize he's not such a bad guy and everyone gets along fine!

ALAN. Red or green, Tommy?

TOMMY. Red.

ALAN. A whopping five! (*Applause and the Studio Audience counts.*) And you land on ... Go To Jail.

TOMMY. I didn't do anything!

ELANA. Technically, you're right.

ALAN. But Dwight was shoplifting and you were with him ... so you were hauled off to jail too.

TOMMY. But I didn't even know he was doing it!

ALAN. But the police didn't believe you and took you in.

ELANA. You only spent two hours there, but your dad had to come and get you.

TOMMY. Man!!!

ALAN. Plus you lose a turn and two points.

TOMMY. But I didn't do anything! This isn't fair!

ELANA. No one said Puberty was fair, Tommy.

ALAN. Here's your chance to get some points, Karen. Pick a card.

KAREN. Green.

ALAN. Another five spacer! (*Applause and counting.*) And you land on Unexpected Turn of Events!

ELANA. Whoa, that also puts you near the end of Puberty!

ALAN. Right you are, Elana.

ELANA. Question or Experience?

KAREN. I'll take the Experience.

ELANA. If you get this Experience correct you will

take the lead, so good luck. Your category is Unexpected Turn of Events and your Experience is: What Do They Really Think? (*Karen walks toward the Experience Circle as two Studio Audience/Inner Thoughts bring chairs into the Circle and sit on the floor behind them. Tommy is "magically" pulled into the Circle.*)

TOMMY. Whoooooaaaa! Hey, what's going on? This isn't my Experience!

ELANA. Actually Tommy, it is partially your Experience. (*Karen sits on one of the chairs, Tommy is pulled onto the other.*)

KAREN. Where are your parents?

KAREN'S INNER VOICE. He looked so cute when he lost at Puberty.

TOMMY. They're finishing signing some papers so I can get my prizes.

TOMMY'S INNER VOICE. I can't believe I she reached Puberty before I did!

KAREN. These game shows really give you nice parting gifts.

KAREN'S INNER VOICE. I think he's still upset.

TOMMY. Yeah.

TOMMY'S INNER VOICE. Yeah, you get to go through puberty and I get the home version, plus a years supply of zit pads.

KAREN. Are you going right back to New Hampshire?

KAREN'S INNER VOICE. I kinda like him. I wonder if he likes me?

TOMMY. I think my family is going to stay here for a week or so. Sort of a vacation.

TOMMY'S INNER VOICE. Why is she looking at me like that?

KAREN. What are you going to do?

KAREN'S INNER VOICE. Why is he looking at me like that?

TOMMY. Oh, I don't know. Go to Disneyland, Universal Studios, Knott's, you know, the touristy stuff.

TOMMY'S INNER VOICE. I wonder if she'd like to go with me?

KAREN. I love Disneyland. I've been there like eight times.

KAREN'S INNER VOICE. Oh, God, don't act like a show off.

TOMMY. I've never been there.

TOMMY'S INNER VOICE. Show off.

KAREN. It'd be fun to show you around.

KAREN'S INNER VOICE. I wonder if he'd ask me to go with him?

TOMMY. Yeah, it would.

TOMMY'S INNER VOICE. I bet mom and dad would let me ask her.

KAREN. My dad even lives in Redondo Beach so I could stay there over the weekend if I went with you.

KAREN'S INNER VOICE. Hello! Testing, testing. Can't you see I'm trying to tell you something here!?

TOMMY. I'll ask my parents.

TOMMY'S INNER VOICE. She's really cute.

KAREN. Great! I'll ask my mom if I can go.

KAREN'S INNER VOICE. Maybe we can ride a romantic ride like Pirates of the Caribbean. (*Tommy sneezes. Tommy's Inner Voice sneezes, too.*)

KAREN AND KAREN'S INNER VOICE. Bless you.

TOMMY AND TOMMY'S INNER VOICE. Thanks.

TOMMY'S INNER VOICE. Boy, I hope I don't have a big old booger hanging out of my nose.

KAREN. Want a Kleenex?

KAREN'S INNER VOICE. He even sneezes cute.

TOMMY. Yeah, thanks. (*She hands him a Kleenex.*)

TOMMY'S INNER VOICE. I knew it. (*Tommy wipes his nose.*) I hope I got it. (*Kevin walks up with a Kevin's Inner Voice behind him.*)

KEVIN. Hey loser, Mom and Dad are finished, we've got to pick up your zit pads and get out of here.

KEVIN INNER VOICE. Poor guy lost to a girl.

TOMMY. Okay, yeah. Ah, Kevin this is Karen.

TOMMY'S INNER VOICE. Please Kevin, don't say anything stupid about me.

KEVIN. Yeah, I just watched the show. Hi, Karen.

KEVIN'S INNER VOICE. I think the little dorkbrain has a crush on her.

KAREN. Nice meeting you.

KAREN'S INNER VOICE. Go away so we can say goodbye.

KEVIN. Yeah, well, we're about to go, so you better finish up, okay?

KEVIN'S INNER VOICE. I'm outta here. (*He leaves with his Inner Voice.*)

TOMMY. Well, I gotta go.

TOMMY'S INNER VOICE. I wonder if I could kiss her?

KAREN. Don't you need my phone number?

KAREN'S INNER VOICE. I wonder if I should kiss him?

TOMMY. Sure.

TOMMY'S INNER VOICE. Oh, man this stuff makes me nervous.

KAREN. It's J-K-L-M-N-O-P.

KAREN'S INNER VOICE. Let's see if he can figure it out.

TOMMY. 555-6667?

TOMMY'S INNER VOICE. Good work Tommy!

KAREN. Yeah. (*Tommy lean over and kisses her on the cheek. Karen is a little surprised.*)

KAREN'S INNER VOICE. Good work Tommy!

TOMMY. I'll call you tonight. (*He exits the Experience Circle with his Inner Voice.*)

TOMMY'S INNER VOICE. Bye. (*Karen sighs. Her Inner Voice sighs too. Babs rings the bell.*)

ALAN. Six points for Karen! (*A horn honk from Babs.*) And that horn tells us were out of time! So the score stands: twenty points for Tommy and twenty-one points for Karen!

ELANA. Which means, Karen, you've made it through Puberty! (*Wild applause.*)

ALAN. Congratulations Karen! You are embarking on an exciting "next step" in your life ... Young Adulthood! Looking forward to it?

KAREN. (*Excited.*) I sure am Alan.

ELANA. (*Standing with Tommy.*) Well, Tommy, you're no doubt a bit disappointed, but don't worry we have some lovely parting gifts. Tell us about them, won't you

Babs?

BABS. (*Music comes up.*) I sure will, Elana. Tommy will receive a case of Zit Zap Pads, the sixty-four ounce bottle of Passion Pit armpit gel, a bottle of Elana Wanna and the home version of Puberty!

ALAN. Well, you really can ask for anything more, now can you?

ELANA. I don't see how you could, Alan.

ALAN. So this is Alan Beckman ...

ELANA. ... and Elana King ...

ALAN. ... saying join us tomorrow ...

ELANA. ... because no one wants to go through Puberty alone.

ALAN. Goodbye!

ELANA. Bye!

BABS. All contestants are under medical supervision while going through Puberty. And don't forget to play Video Puberty! by Nintendo. Now you're playing with power! Puberty! is the registered trademark of Atkins Inc. Now stay tuned for your local news.

• • •

**THE DULLSVILLE MYSTERY**

Comedy. Kim Esop Wylie. Cast of 15 (8-11f, 4-7m) Minimal props, no set required. Dullsville — a town on the brink of terminal boredom. But when a crime of teenage angst explodes, the town is catapulted into an epic whodunit. Who can fathom this most heinous of crimes? How can anyone in their right mind steal another person's gym shorts? No one can be safe in their homes and no one is innocent. Yet in the mire of the investigation, a romance blossoms, true identities are revealed, and strange birthmarks are uncovered. This is a thorough lampooning of high school, adults, small towns, school lunches, crime, and everything in between. It's a show that's fun for actors and audiences alike.